Music
with
Mr Plinkerton

Written and illustrated by
Eleanor Gamper

Ward Lock Educational

&

International Music Publications

Acknowledgements

We are grateful to the following authors and publishers for permission to reproduce these songs.

Clock and watch (What does the clock in the hall say?) from *Music for the Nursery School* by Linda Chesterman, (Harrap Ltd).

Hey ho, here we go from *Fifty Nursery Songs* by Zoltan Kodály, adapted and arranged by Percy M Young with a new English translation by Geoffry Russell-Smith, (Boosey & Hawkes Music Publishers Ltd, 1970).

Long legs, long legs from *Fingers & Thumbs* by Ann Elliott, (Stainer & Bell Ltd).

To and fro (My broom) from *Little Songs with Rhythmic Movement* by Jennifer Day, (Paxton Music Ltd).

Songs & rhymes with words and music by Eleanor Gamper

Sweeping; Cold weather song; My ticking clock; Swing the rope; Shoes; Wind in the trees; Dinosaur; Stairs; Silly Cyril Centipede; The people band; Machines; Mr Plinkerton says; Birthday party; Man with a hat; Girl with a ball; Little green frog; Pigs in the bathroom; Worm in a hole; Baby with a rattle; Rhyme for Easter; Knock on the door; Bangers and mash; Jogging on the spot; Grizzly bears; Toys to sell; Police car; Ding dong; Where are you going, little bear?; Plant a bean.

First published 1986 by
Ward Lock Educational
47 Marylebone Lane
London W1M 6AX

A member of the Ling Kee Group
LONDON · HONG KONG · NEW YORK
SINGAPORE · TAIPEI

© (text and illustrations) 1986 Eleanor Gamper

International Music Publications
Woodford Trading Estate, Southend Road
Woodford Green
Essex IG8 8HN

British Library Cataloguing in Publication Data

Gamper, Eleanor
  Music with Mr. Plinkerton.
  1. Music
  I. Title
  780   ML160

  ISBN 0-7062-4651-9

Designed and illustrated by Eleanor Gamper
Cover photograph by Fiona Pragoff.
Typeset by Dorchester Typesetting Limited.
Printed by Dotesios Printers Limited, Bradford-on-Avon.

Contents

Introduction

In 'Music with Mr Plinkerton' I have set out to identify those skills which are fundamental to a real understanding of music and to offer the teacher or parent a range of ideas and possibilities for developing and extending those skills in the young child, some of which relate specifically to music, but many of which are developing in relation to a wide variety of areas — for instance, number work, reading, social co-operation and physical co-ordination.

The book outlines broad musical concepts such as pulse, rhythm, pitch and dynamics taking them right back to their germinal beginnings. Often the starting point lies within the child himself, in the rhythm of his own body, with the range of sounds he is able to make with his own voice, with his own developing ability to listen to and identify sounds, to discriminate between them and to match them to other sounds. It starts where the child is, learning to live in a social setting, still needing to acquire the skills of group co-operation, patience in taking turns, listening to and conversing with others.

Attention is therefore directed away from tuned instruments, such as the piano, towards a vocal approach to music, where the child must really listen in order to be able to reproduce musical sounds accurately. The emphasis is on helping the child to think musically and to develop his inner ear so that when he eventually comes to learn an instrument it will be with a much more fluent and understanding approach than the usual somewhat mechanical fashion in which instruments such as the piano are so often tackled.

Today's child is exposed to more noise than at any previous point in the history of the world: noise from which there is rarely ever the possibility of escape. With the advent of the electronic media, the sheer quantity of music and other sounds being offered daily (of whatever quality) makes it vital that right from the earliest possible moment we should consciously seek to foster critical listening and discrimination in our children. By that I do not mean that we should force them into the idea that, for instance, 'classical music is good, pop music is rubbish': after all, one can enjoy the aesthetic qualities of both a Rembrandt and an attractive piece of wallpaper. It does help, however, if one can differentiate between the two!

I believe that indiscriminate listening is like a drug: it reduces the listener to a state of mental indifference and passivity. We should not underestimate the serious extent to which the environment of today's child is polluted with noise. I recommend that all music sessions be held in as quiet circumstances as it is humanly possible to provide within the setting of school or playgroup. Many children do not appreciate the meaning of 'peace and quiet' because they have *never* experienced it (except as something Mum is constantly begging them to let her have!). Music time can provide a peaceful haven from the everyday hurly burly of noise. To be able to stop and listen, *really listen*, to oneself as well as others is indeed therapy.

Just as it is important that music-making should be an enjoyable, spontaneous and creative activity for the young child, it is also important that the teacher, whether or not she has a specialist music training, should have a structured approach to the subject and a clear idea of what she is hoping to achieve and how.

I believe that music provides a wonderful opportunity to develop crucial skills in the child which will also equip him or her to perform and cope better in all sorts of other areas. Music is thus lifted out of the category of specialist side-dish for gourmet consumption only and into the main course of essential nourishment for all.

Starting points

Music starts within our own bodies. The first sounds we hear and feel as we lie secure in our mother's womb are the strong pulse of her heartbeat, the quicker flutter of our own tiny hearts, the swoosh of blood being pumped around the body, safe, secure and life-giving. Born into a world of bright light and loud noise, of new, raw sensual experience, we find comfort and security in repetitive rhythm. Our mothers rock us rhythmically, pat us rhythmically. We suck milk rhythmically. We are bounced on mummy or daddy's knee as they sing to us, count our fingers and toes, help us to clap our hands. These are all rhythmic, physical experiences which help to strengthen the bond between us and our parents. Then, as we grow, we learn to rock ourselves, to develop our own comfort and pleasure rhythms.

Even if we never learn to fully appreciate melody, harmony and the complex variety of rhythm, there must be few of us who do not respond spontaneously to repetitive rhythm, whether we dance, tap a foot or a finger, or simply flex the odd muscle. For pulse is built into us, in our heartbeat, our breathing, our walking and running. Duple time is more fundamentally understood than triple for the simple reason that it relates so closely to the symmetry of our own bodies.

So, when teaching music to the young child, it seems logical to start at this instinctive level, with singing games and action rhymes that involve regular, repetitive rhythm, for the child has already come to associate this with security, comfort and pleasure. If he is to learn to 'tune in' to the ordered world of music, he must first learn to tune in to himself, to be aware of the rhythm that is within him in everyday activities and to attempt physical co-ordination and fluency in the simplest of actions.

It is important also to remember that, especially in the very young child, the vocal range is likely to be quite limited, from around the D above middle C to the B above middle C, and that initially he may well have no idea whether a note is high or low, or whether a melodic progression is moving upwards or downwards.

In my work with pre-school children, I have found that invariably they are better able to hear these differences in the human voice than in an instrument, especially one with a wide pitch range such as the piano. For, even though their understanding of basic musical concepts may be very limited, they have already learned how to obtain a great deal of sophisticated information from listening to the human voice, especially as it is frequently augmented by visual gestures, which may be as subtle as the raising of an eyebrow but which nonetheless can help convey a sense of up or down.

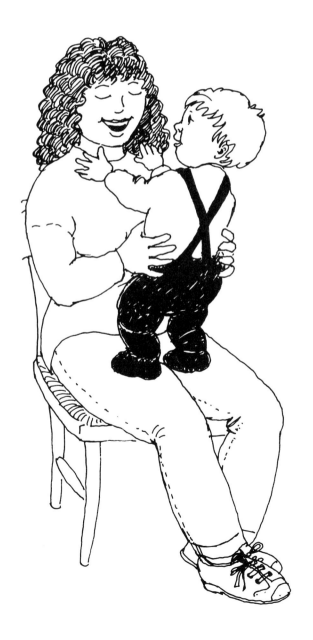

Pulse

If the young child is to progress from purely instinctive reaction to a real understanding of rhythm in all its complexity, then the early sense of pleasure, comfort and security which he finds in rhythm and movement, especially repetitive rhythm and movement, needs to be harnessed and guided into deliberate activity.

An early understanding of the idea of pulse in music, that is, the beat or regular stress that runs throughout, is essential for a later understanding of beats in a bar, rests and time signatures. To be able to feel and count the underlying pulse of a piece of music and to appreciate its continuity behind the variety of different rhythms which may be played against it, is a fundamental skill which needs to be mastered before even the most elementary reading of notation is attempted.

The best way of introducing this idea to children is through a wide variety of action songs and rhymes which involve regular rhythmic movement, such as marching, chopping, sawing, ticking, swinging, etc.

In this chapter I have included suggestions for well known songs which may well be a little outside the young child's actual vocal range. However, I feel that this is offset by the advantage of starting off with something familiar, and initially I am more concerned with establishing a feel for pulse through strong repetitive actions than with achieving perfect singing straight away. Some familiar songs may possibly be adapted to avoid any big vocal leaps, or it may prove easier for the children simply to chant the words.

The words 'beat' and 'pulse' can be introduced to the children as 'special words'. They need to be explained carefully. A possible way would be to say that 'beat' means 'hit': when we hammer our shoes in *Cobbler, cobbler, mend my shoe*, we are hammering the beat. When a policeman walks round the streets making sure all the shops and houses are safely locked up and there are no robbers about, he is 'walking the beat'. This makes a good introduction to *The policeman walks with heavy tread*. You can invite the class to all 'walk the beat together'. Children may have come across the word 'pulse' as something the doctor takes when they are not well. The link can be made here with the heart's beat: it goes on and on whatever we are doing.

Any new 'special words' should be reiterated as often as possible in various different contexts to ensure that the children really understand them. For example, ask them to clap or stamp the pulse, which can then lead on to clapping and counting, or clapping and stressing the first beat of the bar in some way, such as slapping thighs.

Repeating 'One, two, three, four, One, two, three, four, One, two, three, four,' etc. may sound like an incredibly boring activity but small children love it! The younger ones especially like to prove that they can count up to four. They also enjoy lining up and marching while you chant 'One, two, One, two', or 'Left, right, Left, right!'

Activity

Get the children to draw round their feet onto paper and cut them out. (If you're feeling really ambitious you can make real paint footprints.) These can then be stuck round the wall or floor to make a 'marching feet' frieze. You might like to get the children to number the feet: 1, 2, 1, 2, etc.

Walking the beat

Activity

Make 'Daddy Longlegs' and 'Baby Pitter Patter' finger puppets out of thin card. Stick to the back of your hands with grab-tabs or double-sided sellotape so that the daddy has long legs and the baby has short legs. Make them stride, or run with little steps, for the song 'Long Legs, Long Legs'.

Long legs, long legs

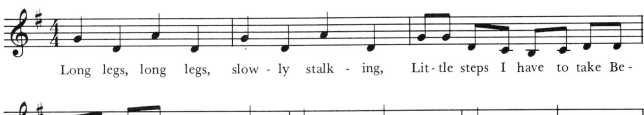

Long legs, long legs, slow-ly stalk-ing, Lit-tle steps I have to take Be-

cause I have such lit-tle feet. See the grown-up peo-ple walk-ing,

Lit-tle ones in lit-tle shoes Go pit-ter, pat-ter down the street.

Long legs, long legs, slowly stalking,   *(take long slow steps)*
Little steps I have to take   *(take tiny quick steps)*
Because I have such little feet.

See the grown up people walking,   *(as first line)*
Little ones in little shoes   *(as second line)*
Go pitter patter down the street.

Poster 1
P. 52

I went to school one morning and I walked like this

I went to school one morn-ing and I walked like this,

Walked like this, walked like this. I went to school one morn-ing and I

walked like this, All on my way to school.

I went to school one morning and I walked like this,
Walked like this, walked like this.
I went to school one morning and I walked like this,
All on my way to school.

The policeman

Walking the beat, walking the beat,
I'm keeping an eye on the things in the street,
And nodding 'hello' to the people I meet,
Walking the beat, walking the beat.

Hammering the beat

Peter hammers with one hammer

Pet - er ham-mers with one ham-mer, One ham-mer, one ham-mer,

Pet - er ham-mers with one ham-mer, All day long.

Peter hammers with one hammer,   *bang on floor with one fist*
One hammer, one hammer,
Peter hammers with one hammer
All day long.

Peter hammers with two hammers,   *two fists*
Two hammers, two hammers,
Peter hammers with two hammers
All day long.

Peter hammers with three hammers, etc.   *fists and one foot*
Peter hammers with four hammers, etc.   *fists and both feet*

Cobbler, cobbler, mend my shoe

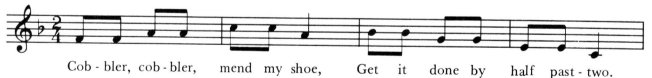

Cob - bler, cob - bler, mend my shoe, Get it done by half past - two.

My toe is peep - ing through, Cob - bler, cob - bler, mend my shoe.

Cobbler, cobbler, mend my shoe,
Get it done by half past two.
My toe is peeping through,
Cobbler, cobbler mend my shoe.

*Children sit cross legged in a circle and
hammer on their shoes.*

Poster 2
P. 54

See-saws

Hey ho, here we go

Hey, ho, Here we go, Up and down and high and low Ri-ding on a see - saw.

Hey, ho,
Here we go,
Up and down and high and low,
Riding on a see-saw.

Children get into pairs and move up and down as if on a see-saw. This is a useful song for introducing so-mi later.

up!

down!

Sweeping the pulse

To and fro, to and fro

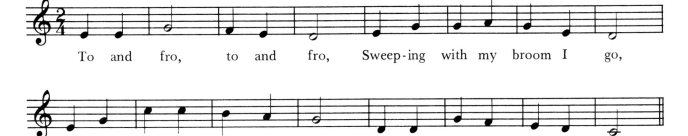

To and fro, to and fro, Sweep-ing with my broom I go,

All the fall - en leaves I sweep, In a big and ti - dy heap.

To and fro, to and fro,
Sweeping with my broom I go,
All the fallen leaves I sweep,
In a big and tidy heap.

Children walk round sweeping rhythmically.

8

Sweeping

Swish, swish, swish, swish, Sweep-ing with my broom, Swish, swish, swish, swish, Sweep-ing up my room. I've sharp-ened pen-cils, eat-en crisps, And cut my ted-dy's hair, But Mum-my says my lit-tle bits are Get-ting ever-y-where. Swish, swish, swish, swish, Sweep-ing with my broom, Swish, swish, swish, swish, Sweep-ing up my room.

Swish, swish, swish, swish,
Sweeping with my broom,
Swish, swish, swish, swish,
Sweeping up my room.
I've sharpened pencils, eaten crisps,
And cut my teddy's hair,
But Mummy says my little bits are
Getting everywhere.
Swish, swish, swish, swish
Sweeping with my broom,
Swish, swish, swish, swish,
Sweeping up my room.

Children mime sweeping.

Other possibilities
*Use 'swish swish swish swish' as an ostinato
(spoken or chanted rather than sung) against
the tune.*

Poster 3
P. 56

swish   swish   swish   swish

swish   swish   swish   swish

Rowing the pulse

Row, row, row your boat

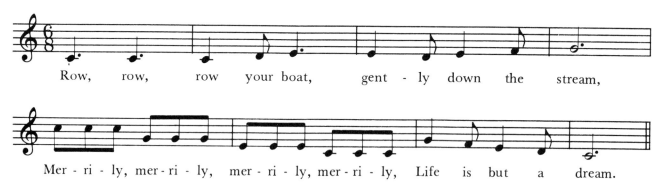

Row,   row,   row   your boat,   gent - ly   down   the   stream,

Mer - ri - ly, mer - ri - ly, mer - ri - ly, mer - ri - ly, Life   is   but   a   dream.

Row, row, row your boat, gently down the stream,
Merrily, merrily, merrily, merrily,
Life is but a dream.

Children sit on the floor and pretend to row. It is less easy for them to keep the pulse steady if they do it in pairs as is sometimes suggested for this song.

Try it with half the group chanting '*Heave*-ho, *Heave*-ho' while the rest sing the verse.

Sawing the beat

If it is decided to vary the actions or the songs, make sure that the actions, whatever they are, are regular, repetitive ones that will illustrate the idea of pulse as opposed to rhythm.

We are woodmen sawing trees

Children pretend to saw. Try to get them to saw down on the down beat.

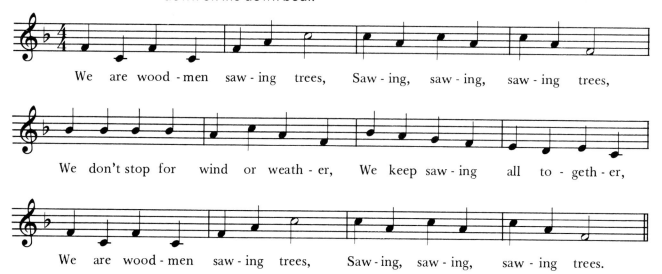

We   are   wood - men   saw - ing   trees,   Saw - ing,   saw - ing,   saw - ing   trees,

We   don't stop   for   wind   or   weath - er,   We   keep saw - ing   all   to - geth - er,

We   are   wood - men   saw - ing   trees,   Saw - ing,   saw - ing,   saw - ing   trees.

We are woodmen sawing trees,
Sawing, sawing, sawing trees,
We don't stop for wind or weather,
We keep sawing all together;
We are woodmen sawing trees,
Sawing, sawing, sawing trees.

Stamping and clapping

When I do this with my class I like to put up a picture of stamping feet and clapping hands. Once we have really established the pulse I point to the pictures, using them as a form of rhythm notation. This can then develop into a game: I point to the stamping feet and the children have to stamp the beat; I then point to the hands and they have to change from stamping to clapping. This is done without singing the tune although it can be sung to 'la'. (However, this is quite difficult to do at the same time as clapping, stamping and looking at pictures.)

Notation ideas

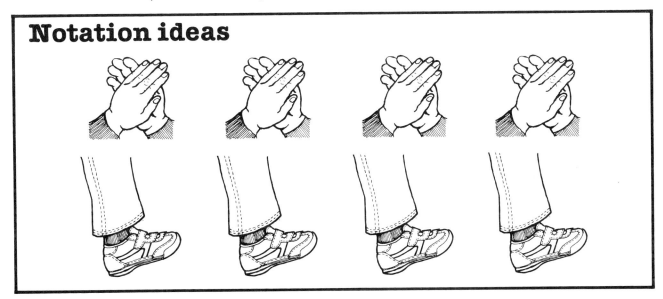

Cold weather song

When it's cold we clap our hands, We clap our hands, We clap our hands,

When it's cold we clap our hands, We clap our hands like this.

Poster 4
P. 58

When it's cold we clap our hands,
We clap our hands,
We clap our hands,
When it's cold we clap our hands,
We clap our hands like this.

When it's cold we stamp our feet,
We stamp our feet,
We stamp our feet,
When it's cold we stamp our feet,
We stamp our feet like this.

Ticking clocks

Hickory dickory dock,
The mouse ran up the clock,
The clock struck one,
The mouse ran down,
Hickory, dickory, dock.

Children will be fascinated if you show them a metronome. Set it ticking at about 88 and get them to join in, chanting 'tick-tock' and moving their arms like the metronome. Explain that it is 'ticking out the pulse'.

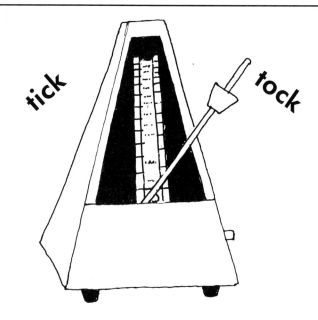

My ticking clock

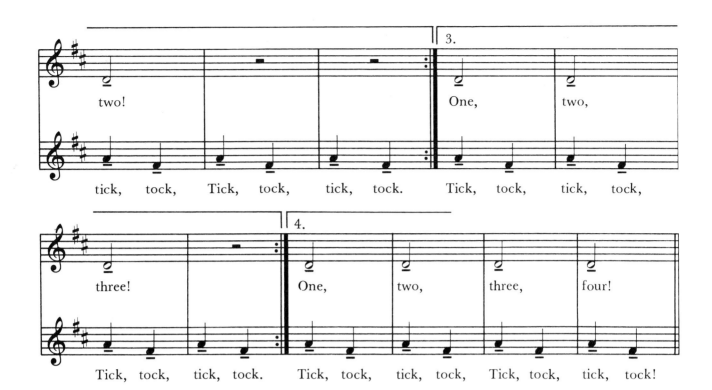

two! One, two,

tick, tock, Tick, tock, tick, tock. Tick, tock, tick, tock,

three! One, two, three, four!

Tick, tock, tick, tock. Tick, tock, tick, tock, Tick, tock, tick, tock!

Can you hear my ticking clock,
Ticking out the time?
When it gets to one o'clock,
You will hear it chime,
One!

Can you hear my ticking clock,
Ticking out the time?
When it gets to two o'clock,
You will hear it chime,
One, two!

Can you hear my ticking clock,
Ticking out the time?
When it gets to three o'clock,
You will hear it chime,
One, two, three!

Can you hear my ticking clock,
Ticking out the time?
When it gets to four o'clock,
You will hear it chime,
One, two, three four!

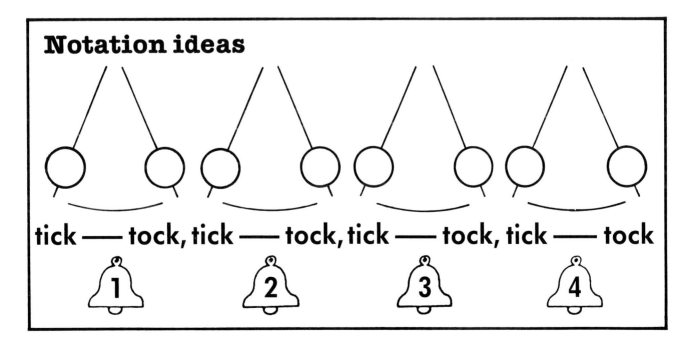

Notation ideas

tick — tock, tick — tock, tick — tock, tick — tock

What does the clock in the hall say?

What does the clock in the hall say?
Tick, tock, tick, tock,
What does the clock on the wall say?
Tick, tick, tick, tick, tick, tick, tick, tick,
What do little watches all say?
Tick-a, tick-a, tick-a, tick-a, tick-a, tick-a, tick.

Children swing their arms like a pendulum for the first line, from side to side like a metronome for the clock on the wall, and tap fingers on wrists for the little watches.

Rhythm against pulse

Having introduced a number of songs where the regular actions reinforce the pulse, all sorts of other songs can be introduced where the children clap or tap the pulse whilst singing or chanting the rhythm, so that they can appreciate the difference between the two. With very young children, the business of clapping and singing at the same time is a bit like patting your head and rubbing your tummy at the same time, so songs need to be simple and rhythmically obvious. It helps if they are already well known to the children.

Clap the pulse and sing the song
Try some of these:

Polly put the kettle on
Sing a song of sixpence
I had a little nut tree
London Bridge is falling down

Poster 5
P. 60

Pease pudding hot
Baa baa black sheep
The grand old Duke of York
One, two, three, Mother caught a flea
Here we go round the mulberry bush
Pop goes the weasel

I hear thunder, I hear thunder;
Hark, don't you?
Hark, don't you?
Pitter-patter raindrops,
Pitter-patter raindrops,
I'm wet through –
SO ARE YOU!

One, two, three, four,
Mary at the cottage door,
Eating cherries off a plate,
Five, six, seven, eight.

Poster 6
P. 62

What rhythm are the raindrops telling us?

Can you clap it?

Try whispering 'pitter patter' all the way through the song.

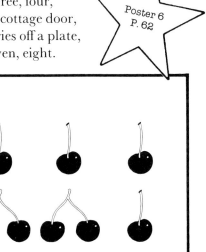

Can you guess the rhyme?

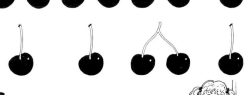

Using instruction cards

If the children enjoy the ticking clocks exercises, you might like to develop the idea further. Divide them into two groups, one to sing the verse and the other to sing, chant or clap 'tick, tock,' according to their ability. I find it useful to hand out little 'instruction cards': it lends an air of excitement (which card will they get?) and it develops the idea of instructions being conveyed in written or visual form. Later, when children have got used to the idea of instruction cards you can use cards with more abstract symbols on them such as **p** for soft and **f** for loud.

means *sing the verse*

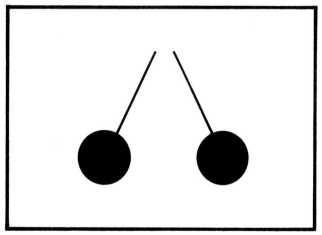

means *sing 'tick, tock,'*
(or chant)
(or clap)

This is a difficult exercise for young children, so do not expect instant results.

Skipping rhymes

A very good source of material for rhythmic work is our variety of skipping and other traditional playground rhymes and chants. It could make quite an interesting project for older children in the school to make a collection of the playground chants common in the school. These are under threat from TV jingles and the 'top ten' but it is surprising how many survive, becoming modified with each new generation.

You are not likely to find a four-year-old who can skip, but many four-year-olds wish they could skip and will enjoy jumping up and down pretending to do so whilst chanting a simple rhyme such as:

> Salt,
> Mustard,
> Vinegar,
> *Pepper!*

Skipping games which involve two children swinging the rope whilst the others skip in single or double time are a wonderful example of co-ordinated rhythmic activity. The pulse is *felt*, through the physical action of swinging the rope and jumping; it is *seen*, as the children watch the rope swing to and fro or round and round; it is *heard*, as the children chant the different, sometimes quite complex rhythms against it.

It is extremely important to use as much material as can be found, from whatever sources available, to develop children's physical rhythmic fluency and co-ordination. This fluency is fundamental to the development of musical skills (and probably a lot of others, such as language, reading and numeracy).

Swing the rope

A pretend skipping game in which two children mime the action of swinging the rope and the others skip over it.

Swing the rope
Round and round,
See how your feet
Touch the ground,
One and two and
How-do-you-do,
O.U.T. spells *out*!   *children jump out on the word 'out'*

Shoes
Children walk round, pretending to wear the
various different kinds of shoes.

I've got Daddy's slippers on,   *large strides*
Slip slop slip slop,
I've got frogman's flippers on,
Flip flop flip flop,
I've got Mummy's high-heeled shoes on,
Clitter clatter clitter clatter,   *small, quicker steps*
I've got baby's woolly boots on,
Pitter patter pitter patter.

Poster 7
P.64

I've got Daddy's slippers on,

Slip, slop, slip, slop,

I've got frogman's flippers on,

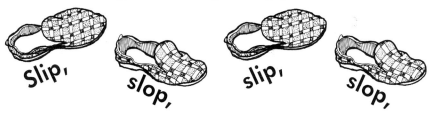

Flip, flop, flip, flop,

I've got Mummy's high-heeled shoes on,

Clit-ter, clat-ter, clit-ter, clat-ter,

I've got Baby's woolly boots on,

Pit-ter, pat-ter, pit-ter, pat-ter.

An old playground chant which is still going strong in the playground of my old school is 'Join on for more men'. This is a recruitment game, usually for boys who want to form a large enough group for a game of what would have been cowboys and indians in my day but is probably star wars or battle of the planets by now. Children march round the playground, arms around each other's shoulders until a long line is formed. If you have plenty of space it provides another activity for 'walking the beat'. Get the children who are waiting to join on the end of the line to come in on the word 'join', which will make the whole thing more rhythmically co-ordinated.

Notation idea

Join   on   for   more   men.

Listening

Music is primarily about two activities: listening to and making sound. In this age of noise pollution children learn to blot out noise to survive. They may never have stopped to really listen and be aware of the sounds they hear. Yet there is such a mass of information that can be gained simply by listening.

Activity

Ask the class to really listen. Suggest that they close their eyes to help them concentrate. Talk about what they can hear, and make a list of all the different sounds. Try moving around the school, out into the playground, etc. Make a picture of the sounds you hear: perhaps a montage using cut out pictures from magazines, or the children's own drawings.

Play a 'sound detective' game: Collect a number of familiar items which make a sound. Hide them behind a screen and see who can identify them by their sound. Or for a really sophisticated version make a tape recording, which will enable you to get a lot more 'location noises' such as running water, traffic, road drills, etc.

Poster 8
P.66

Loud-soft

Quiet sounds

You will need quiet surroundings for this: Try to eliminate as much external noise as possible. It is important that the children are not distracted or prevented from hearing altogether. Sit in a circle, as close together as possible so that everyone can hear you. Start by experimenting with the different sorts of quiet sounds that it is possible to make with our own bodies. For example, rubbing hands together; rubbing finger nails together; tapping fingers on your palm; tapping your head or your teeth (sounds louder to the tapper), etc. Some children are bound to make loud instead of soft sounds which presents the opportunity of discussing and evaluating what is 'loud' and what is 'soft'.

Still working on the theme of quiet body sounds, you can develop a game where everyone shuts his eyes. One person makes a sound and the others have to try and reproduce the sound as closely as they can. Another variation is to start a steady pulse going using a quiet body sound and get everyone to come in with their sounds in time to your pulse.

Activity

Make 'quiet shakers' from sheets of newspaper. Roll up the paper and fix with *sticky tape. Make about six cuts lengthwise and pull out as for a paper tree.*

pull out, holding the centre

roll firmly as this forms the 'handle'

cut about 7" down

Make a paper 'orchestra': Each child has a sheet of paper, about 6"×4" and one or two paper shakers.

Wind in the trees

The wind is starting to blow.	*Rub the sheet of paper quite slowly with your hand.*
The rain is falling on the leaves.	*Drum fingers lightly on the paper.*
Now the wind is getting stronger and the branches are moving.	*Rub the paper more quickly.*
And now the whole tree is swaying in the wind.	*Rustle the shakers.*
	Now sway from side to side, rustling the shakers and whispering this rhyme:

> Blow, blow, blow the wind,
> Gently in the trees,
> Louder and louder it blows and then,
> It fades to a gentle breeze.

For the last two lines rustle the shakers faster to make a crescendo, then die away again. This exercise illustrates the point that you can have a *crescendo* without necessarily being *loud*.

Dinosaur

A rhythmic exercise which contrasts loud and soft through stamping and tiptoeing.

One, two, three, four,
Here comes a dinosaur!
Hear him stomp,
Through the swamp,
Thump, thump, thump, thump!

Let us wait till he's asleep,
Then we'll quietly past him creep
On our toes,
Mind his nose!
Creep, creep, creep, creep.

Pre-notation activity

Make monster footprints out of paper. Large ones can stick on the floor (close enough for the children to stride from one to another and keep the pulse steady).

Later, the rhythm can be written onto them:

One / two / three / four, / Here / comes a / dino- / saur!

Pitch

Introducing notation

I have always used a lot of visual material in my classes: not, I hasten to add, five-line staves plastered with black dots, but right from the very beginning I have found that it can help to reinforce some of the very fundamental musical concepts that the children are forming, such as high – low, up – down, long notes – short notes, notes that are all the same duration, and so on. The use of illustrations and symbols accustoms the child to the idea that sounds can be visually represented in various ways. A wide variety of visual images that are changed frequently also makes an interesting environment in which to make music. Illustrations to songs help the children to call those songs to mind and therefore to hear them in their heads.

Visual symbols for high and low, and physical movement to express musical progression up and down, all help to equip the child with a basic set of mental 'co-ordinates' which may help him to place notes mentally. Also, the more the child is encouraged to use his imagination to conjure up mental images at will, the more it will seem reasonable to conjure up 'sound pictures' as well.

Poster 9 P. 68

Mr Plinkerton walks upstairs,

Then runs back down in case of bears.

Mr Plinkerton is a musical note. Sometimes he likes to go up high and make a high sound and sometimes he likes to come right down and make a low sound.

Mr Plinkerton is rather a useful character. He can be traced onto a bit of card and used like a puppet – to go 'upstairs and downstairs' or even just held up to get the children's attention, for instance: Mr Plinkerton says 'everyone be quiet and listen', etc.

Stairs

Mis - ter Plin - ker-ton walks up - stairs Then runs back down in case of bears.

Mr Plinkerton walks upstairs,
Then runs back down in case of bears.

Make your arm into the stairs. Your other hand is Mr Plinkerton – make him walk upstairs by walking your fingers up your arm, then come back down.

Mr Plinkerton's climbing frame

In this game you are asking the children to try and differentiate between high and low notes. It is best to use your voice for this, or perhaps a glockenspiel. I have found the piano has rather too wide a range for the children to take their pitch accurately.

On a large sheet of thick card (or on paper which you then pin to a board) draw Mr Plinkerton's climbing frame. I like to use one with two sets of five lines on it even though I am only asking the children to make very basic distinctions between high and low. I think it helps to give the visual impression that there are steps in between 'high' and 'low', and one child's idea of 'high' might be very different to another child's idea of 'high'.

Copy or trace Mr Plinkerton and stick him down onto card. Cut him out and fix a lump of 'Blu-tack' to his back. Explain that Mr Plinkerton is a musical note. Sometimes he likes to go 'plink' up high; sometimes he likes to go 'plink' down low, and sometimes he likes to go 'plink' somewhere in the middle. (That is why he is called Mr *Plink*erton!)

Ask the children to listen carefully to the notes you are going to sing or play and tell you whether they are 'high', 'low' or 'somewhere in the middle'.

The children then place Mr Plinkerton in what they feel is the correct position on his climbing frame.

When you have been playing this game for a while there will probably be some discussion about the relative pitch of different notes: are they high, higher or lower? (Another reason for not using the piano for this exercise: a note may be the highest note you can sing but it is still a lot lower than the highest note on the piano.)

A variation on this game, which will be more successful when the children have gained a bit more confidence, is to play it in reverse: you place Mr Plinkerton somewhere on the climbing frame and ask the children to sing where they think he is.

Once they have become accustomed to linking the visual idea of up-down with the sound idea of up-down ask them to close their eyes and imagine Mr Plinkerton's climbing frame, or perhaps a staircase (the one with the bears at the top). Explain that you are going to sing (or play) some notes and you want them to say whether Mr Plinkerton is going up the stairs or coming down the stairs.

Draw the 'climbing frame' onto stout card, or pin paper onto a board.

Make the lines about 10mm thick and leave approximately 40mm space between the lines.

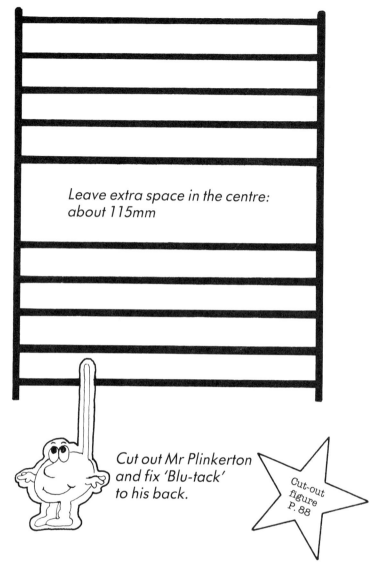

Leave extra space in the centre: about 115mm

Cut out Mr Plinkerton and fix 'Blu-tack' to his back.

Cut-out figure P. 88

Silly Cyril Centipede

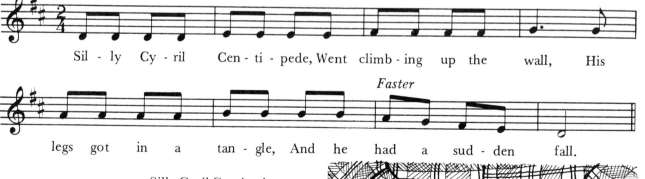

Sil - ly Cy - ril Cen - ti - pede, Went climb - ing up the wall, His

Faster

legs got in a tan - gle, And he had a sud - den fall.

Silly Cyril Centipede,
Went climbing up the wall,
His legs got in a tangle,
And he had a sudden fall.

Children start off crouching down. Using wiggly fingers* to make 'Silly Cyril' they gradually stand up and then come down quickly on the last line, landing with 'Cyril' on his back, 'legs' in the air.

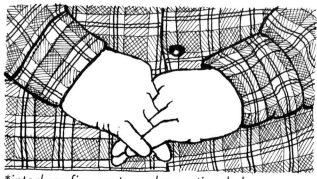

*interlace fingers to make centipede legs

Developing skills

Singing games

Moving on from songs and rhymes with regular repetitive actions, we can introduce children to the world of the singing game, where specific actions have to be performed at the correct point in the song. Singing games perform all sorts of useful functions:

they make singing enjoyable
they foster physical co-ordination and fluency
they encourage intelligent listening
they help children learn to take turns and co-operate within the group

The following singing game continues the idea of different body sounds. It is important that whatever sounds you choose are performed rhythmically.

The People Band

We are the People Band,
When we play it's really grand,
Hear us when we clap our hands,
Clap, clap, clap, clap,
Clap our hands.

Numerous variations can be invented for this song: 'Hear us when we tap our knees; smack our legs; stamp our feet; rub our hands; tap our teeth; pat our cheeks, etc.

Once the children have grasped the idea of this song another variation is to ask them not to sing the fourth line, just clap, tap or whatever, which means that if you are singing the song unaccompanied they will need to hold the tune in their heads in order to come in on the last line. Encourage the children to suggest different sounds for the People Band.

Machines

Children pretend to be different parts of a big machine.

Up, down, up, down, *Move arms up and down.*

Clitter, clatter, clonk! *Stretch arms out sideways and move them up and down.*

In, out, in, out, *Move arms in and out.*

Wiggle, woggle, *bonk*! *Stamp from one foot to the other, with an extra hard stamp on 'bonk!'*

Start by practising each movement separately, then put them together. Once the children have learnt the rhyme they can try getting into small groups, with each group doing a different movement. Bring in yet another element by asking someone to come in with a drum or tambourine on the word '*clonk!*' or *bonk!*'. With older children you may be able to develop the machine idea to the point where the children invent their own repetitive rhythm and movement and perhaps also draw pictures to express it.

Echo games

These exercises are aimed at developing the memory and powers of concentration. They start with copycat games where the children mirror your or each other's movements exactly and progress to echo clapping games in which you clap a short rhythmic phrase to them and they clap it back to you. The regular inclusion of these exercises in your music sessions can yield very good results if you are prepared to persevere in the initial stages, especially if working with pre-school children, who will probably take time to understand what exactly you are asking them to do. The younger the child the shorter the concentration span and the more likely he is to be distracted, or hindered by shyness. Ability to perform well in these exercises obviously increases as the child becomes more proficient at understanding and carrying out instructions, learning to take turns and learning to keep still. Conversely, these echo exercises also help to improve those abilities.

Remember, the important thing to begin with is *keep it simple*! The younger children will take a while to grasp that you want them to actually do anything, let alone perform a complex rhythmic phrase.

These phrases may suggest parts of rhymes or songs to the children.

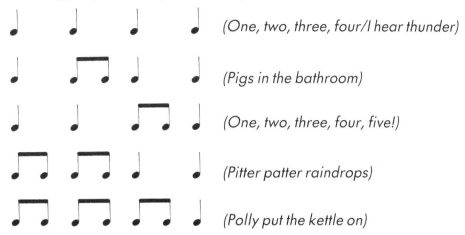

(One, two, three, four/I hear thunder)

(Pigs in the bathroom)

(One, two, three, four, five!)

(Pitter patter raindrops)

(Polly put the kettle on)

Signals

This exercise is intended to give the children practice in understanding and carrying out instructions at a given signal. For example, get them to clap a steady pulse. Devise a hand-signal to mean 'stop', such as rapidly parting your hands, which you explain to them beforehand, and also a signal for 'start clapping' (such as raising your hands). Practise starting and stopping at your signals. This can also be tried with other activities such as marching round. You can also introduce a different visual element by holding up signal cards: for instance, red for stop, green for start, or with very simple symbols such as clapping hands for 'start clapping' and a dash for 'be quiet'.

Signal cards PP.86,87, 88

(Only try these with readers or those with good left-right orientation)

Mr Plinkerton Says . . .

An instructions game rather along the lines of 'O'Grady says' but with rhythmical instructions.

To make this more fun for the children you might like to make a cut-out Mr Plinkerton puppet and hold him up on the line 'Mr Plinkerton says'.

Mis - ter Plin - ker-ton says Clap your hands Mis - ter

Plin - ker-ton says Stamp your feet Mis - ter Plin - ker-ton says Put your

hands up-on your head And go march - ing to the beat.

Mr Plinkerton says,

Clap your hands,   *clap clap*

Mr Plinkerton says,

Stamp your feet,   *stamp stamp*

Mr Plinkerton says,

Put your hands upon your head,

And go marching to the beat.

Mr Plinkerton says,

Tap your knees,   *tap tap*

Mr Plinkerton says,

Point your toes,   *point point*

Turn around,

Make your fingers touch the ground,

Then climb up to your nose.
'walk' fingers up body to nose

Make Mr Plinkerton

Mr Plinkerton is guaranteed to have a magic effect on children. Hold him up. Do a 'Mr Plinkerton' voice: he can tell the children to sit down, sit still, be quiet, put their hands on their heads, ask them if they can sing a song, etc.

Trace or copy Mr Plinkerton and stick him onto a piece of card. Cut out and tape a stick to his back (a short piece of garden cane, a plastic drinking straw, or even a pencil will do).

Birthday party
Choose a child to have a 'birthday'.
Choose a second child to give the 'present'.
The first child stands in the middle while the
others follow the second child, marching
round in a big circle.

(All) Go - ing to a par - ty, Go - ing to a par - ty,

Let's take a pre - sent, What shall we take?

(Giver) I'll give you a (clap clap), (All) We'll give you a (clap clap),

(Receiver) Thank you for my (clap clap), (All) That's all right!

All   Going to a party,
Going to a party,
Let's take a present,
What shall we take?

*The second child steps forward to give the 'present' to the first child. All
stand still for this verse:*

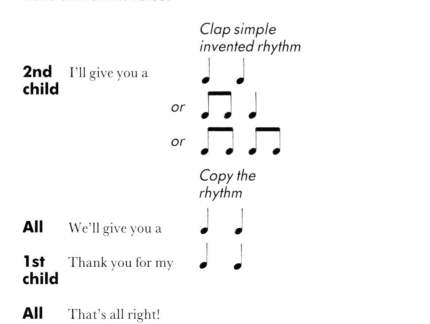

*Clap simple
invented rhythm*

**2nd
child**   I'll give you a

or

or

*Copy the
rhythm*

All   We'll give you a

**1st
child**   Thank you for my

All   That's all right!

Rhythm
cards
PP.84,85

The song is then repeated with different children taking the parts of present givers and receivers. Keep the rhythms very simple. Two quite difficult skills are being attempted here. One is making up a rhythm, which even if the child has the ability, he or she may not have the confidence to perform in front of the others. The other is copying a rhythm accurately.

For this reason the tune is kept very simple – almost a chant.

Silly rhythms

Silly rhythms are a series of rhythmic chants with actions. Encourage the children to make up their own. Each different chant has an 'instruction card' with a picture and notation for the first line of that chant. Use the cards in different ways: hold them up as you chant; use them to tell the children which one to chant next; lay them out and let each child choose one to do as a solo. Get the children to make cards for their own chants.

Man with a hat,

Man with a hat,

Howd'ye-do, howd'ye-do,   *raise hat twice*

Man with a hat.

Girl with a ball,

Girl with a ball,

Bounce! bounce!   *bounce twice*

Girl with a ball.

Little green frog,

Little green frog,

Boing! boing!   *hop twice*

Little green frog.

Pigs in the bathroom,

Pigs in the bathroom,

Splash! splash!   *mime splashing with arms*

Pigs in the bathroom.

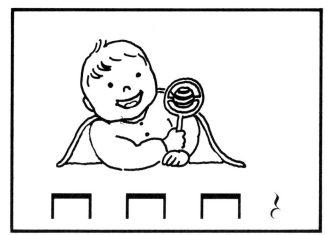

Worm in a hole,

Worm in a hole,

Wriggle-wriggle, wriggle-wriggle,   *wriggle*

Worm in a hole.

A possible extension of this exercise is to clap the rhythms instead of chanting them, still retaining the actions for the third line.

Baby with a rattle,

Baby with a rattle,

Shake, shake, shake, shake,   *mime shaking*

Baby with a rattle.

Clap the rhythm and ask the children to choose the correct card: some of the rhythms are identical so there may be more than one correct answer.

Recognising a tune from its rhythm

Clap the rhythm of a familiar nursery rhyme or song and ask the children to try and recognise the tune you are clapping. If you are in the habit of starting your classes with some well-known songs and rhymes that you use for clapping or walking the beat then these will be fairly fresh in the children's minds. As they get better at this game you might try asking one child to choose a rhyme and clap it for the class and you to guess.

Another version of this game is to choose a well-known rhyme (not a song) and alternately speak and clap each line. It may help at first to suggest that whilst clapping, the children mouth the words: the mouthing provides a bridge between actually hearing and mentally hearing the words.

Holding the tune in your head
A very popular game to try is to clap the pulse for, say, *Baa, baa, black sheep* and sing the song, but mouth every other line. Clapping helps the class to come in together. Do it with them and mouth the words very exaggeratedly so that they can really see that something is

going on when they are not actually making a sound.

Try this game with other well-known nursery rhymes. Later, when the children become more proficient, try leaving out more than one line or, even more difficult, starting silently and getting them to come in on your signal.

As a variation it may help to put up simple notation and point to it as you sing. Again, this reinforces the idea that something musical is going on even when there is silence.

Notation idea

Baa,   baa,   black   sheep,

Yes   sir,   Yes   sir,

Introducing the quarter-note rest

Choose a selection of rhymes where the quarter-note rest can at first be substituted by a positive sound. For instance: in *One two three, mother caught a flea* make the sound and action of a flea hopping where the rest occurs!

> One, two, three, (boing!)
> Mother caught a flea, (boing!)
> Put it in the tea pot and
> Made a cup of tea, (boing!)

> Pease pudding hot (whoo!)
> Pease pudding cold, (brr!)
> Pease pudding in the pot,
> Nine days old (uggh!)

In *Hot cross buns*, make a munching sound where the rest occurs:

> Hot cross buns, (yum!)
> Hot cross buns, (yum!)
> One a penny, two a penny,
> Hot cross buns (yum!)

Poster 11
P. 72

Practise chanting through the rhymes but only whispering the 'rest' words, or just mouthing them. Clap the rhythms and 'throw away' the rests – do this at the same time as you chant the rhythm or on its own.

Put up pictorial notation and point to it as you go along as a visual guide.

Notation idea
Rhyme for Easter

Five   lit-tle   East-er   eggs,

Sit-ting   in a   nest,   (ssh!)

One for   you,   One for   me, My

broth-er   ate the   rest!   (ssh!)

Sssh! I'm having a rest.

What rhythm are the buns telling us?

Try saying 'ssh' instead of 'yum'.

Invite the children to either make a munching sound or say 'yum' when they come to the picture of a person eating (just one – for the duration of a quarter-note). When they have practised this a few times, stick the symbol for a quarter-note rest over the faces. Remind the children about the rest saying 'ssh' and practise the piece again substituting 'ssh' for 'yum' and trying to make it quieter with each successive repeat until they are simply mouthing it (putting fingers to lips at the same time helps).

Although the tune for this is well known, the object of the exercise is to gain an understanding of rhythm notation and it is probably better simply to chant it. Also the octave leaps may well be beyond the children who would be struggling with the melody at the expense of understanding the notation, and gaining a feel for rhythm against pulse. If the children want to try it with the tune later, try substituting so-mi-do for so-so, do, in the first bar.

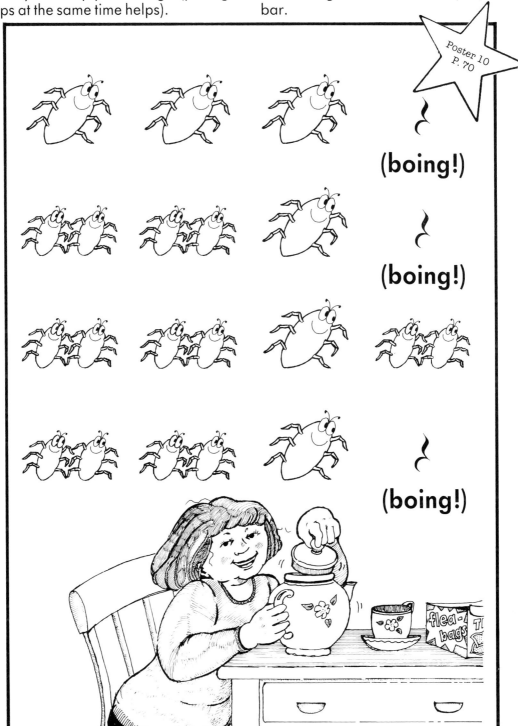

Poster 10
P. 70

(boing!)

(boing!)

(boing!)

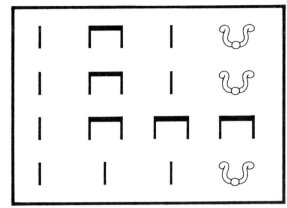

Knock on the door, (knock)
Knock on the door, (knock)
Nobody's answering so
Knock some more (knock).

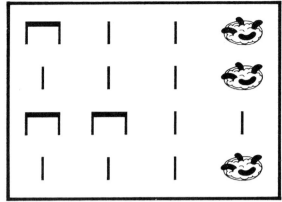

Bangers and mash, (yum)
Corned beef hash, (yum)
Cover it with gravy,
Splash, splash, splash, (uggh!)

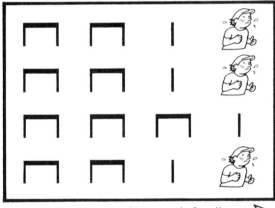

Jogging on the spot, (whoo!)
Jogging on the spot, (whoo!)
All that jogging up and down,
Makes us very hot, (whoo!)

Jog on the spot to this one.

Rhythm
cards
PP. 85, 86

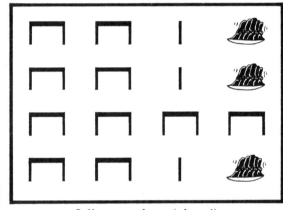

Jelly on a plate, (gloop!)
Jelly on a plate, (gloop!)
Wibble wobble wibble wobble,
Jelly on a plate (gloop!)

Introducing untuned percussion instruments

It is very easy, especially with younger children, for the introduction of percussion instruments to result in an extremely noisy free-for-all in which all the wonderful groundwork you have been doing with them – the clapping, walking, chanting, body rhythms and so on – is totally forgotten, discipline breaks down and you end up resorting to the aspirin bottle!

Obviously children will need to be able to explore the possibilities of various instruments, to examine them and experiment with them. Hopefully many of them will have had this opportunity whilst at playgroup or even at toddler groups. I personally feel it is a good idea to keep the experimental sessions distinct from the more organised music sessions. This is not to say that the experimental sessions should not be organised, and neither is it in any way saying that the 'organised' sessions are not to involve music initiated by the child. If you have just spent some time concentrating on beautiful, accurate rhythm work with your children, helping them to feel the pulse, to hear rhythmic phrases in their heads, to clap and sing in an accurate, co-ordinated way, then what message are you conveying if you suddenly hand out instruments and 'let them get on with it' – that all they have done previously does not count when it comes to playing 'real' instruments?

Experimental sessions involving percussion instruments should be extending the musical concepts that the children have already been forming in early sessions: loud and soft sounds, long and short sounds, etc. Try helping the children to enlarge their vocabulary of words to describe sounds: hard, soft, sad, gentle, etc. Above all they need to discover how to control the sound made by each instrument. Before he can produce accurate rhythm work with an instrument, the child must know how to hold it, how to make a sound with it and how to stop making a sound with it. Some of the traditional percussion instruments most widely held to be suitable for young children are in fact the most difficult to play. Watch a young child trying to make contact with a swinging triangle and see that it would probably be easier to suspend it from a stand for him. Try playing some maraccas, or some yoghurt pots full of split peas and notice how the peas roll about when you shake them, giving a little up-beat to your deliberate down beat.

Guess the instrument

Set up a screen behind which you can conceal a number of different untuned percussion instruments and play them without them being seen by the class.

Onto the screen pin up pictures of the various instruments. You might also choose a short

rhythmic phrase such as ♩ ♫ ♩ ♩ and pin up simplified notation for this onto the screen as well. You then ask the children to listen as you play the short phrase on one of the

instruments and try to guess which one you are playing. It may help to talk about the pictures first, making sure children know the names of the various instruments depicted. When a correct guess is made you can then show the instrument. Then play the phrase again, explaining how the sound is being made, how you are holding the instrument, etc.

An extension of this game is to then play two instruments at once and ask the children to identify them. Or start playing one and get them to put up their hands when the second starts to play. It may be easier to use a tape recorder and pre-record the examples for this game, depending on your dexterity!

When you have exhausted the guessing possibilities, (always playing the same rhythmic phrase), hand out the instruments and try to get the class to repeat that same rhythmic phrase. Again, there are lots of possibilities: each child playing in turn; you clap the phrase, the child plays it back; you call out 'drums' and all the drums play the phrase, and so on.

One of the biggest obstacles to overcome with young children is that of getting them to hold an instrument and *not* play it, especially when it is still a novelty. The cardboard Mr Plinkerton puppet from the instructions game *Mr Plinkerton says* could prove very useful here: Hold him up and try 'Mr Plinkerton says, "Don't make any sounds."' You could develop a *Mr Plinkerton says* game with the instruments along the lines of 'Mr Plinkerton says, "Bang your drum.", "Shake your maraccas like this"'

 and so on.

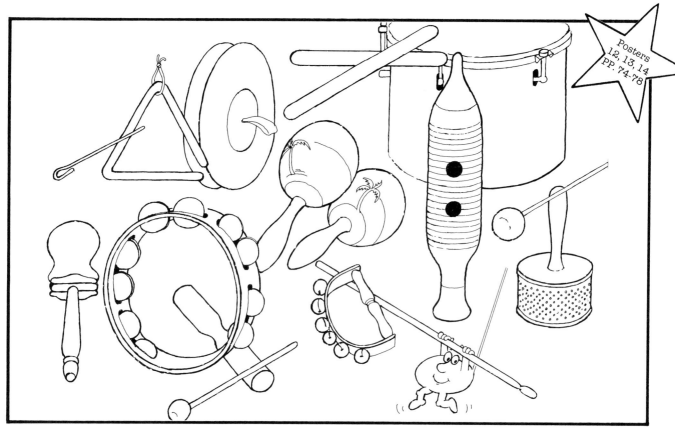

Some simple notation ideas for untuned percussion

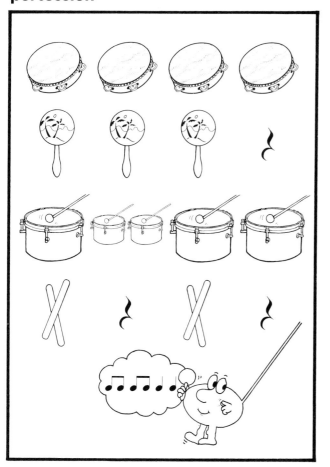

More difficult phrases involving more than one instrument

shake   shake   shake   bang

clink   bang   clink   bang

shake-a   shake-a   shake   ting

Recognising simple pitch relationships

Introducing tonic sol-fa names

Having established a good sense of 'high' and 'low', 'up' and 'down', and having accustomed the children to the idea of notes moving upwards and downwards in steps (as in *Mr Plinkerton goes upstairs* for instance) you can move on to identify some simple pitch relationships using tonic sol-fa names.

Making tonic sol-fa people

Onto stout card draw up a set of steps as shown in the illustration. Cut this out and tape or glue a paper pocket to the back of each step into which can be slotted a small card, (about 4½"×2"). You will need eight of these small cards. Onto each card trace one of the tonic sol-fa characters illustrated, and colour in, making the colours as different as possible.

The steps can either be propped up as in the illustration, by sticking a box to the back, and putting a weight into it, or by pinning it to a board. The tonic sol-fa characters are then slotted into their respective pockets on the steps and you are ready to introduce them.

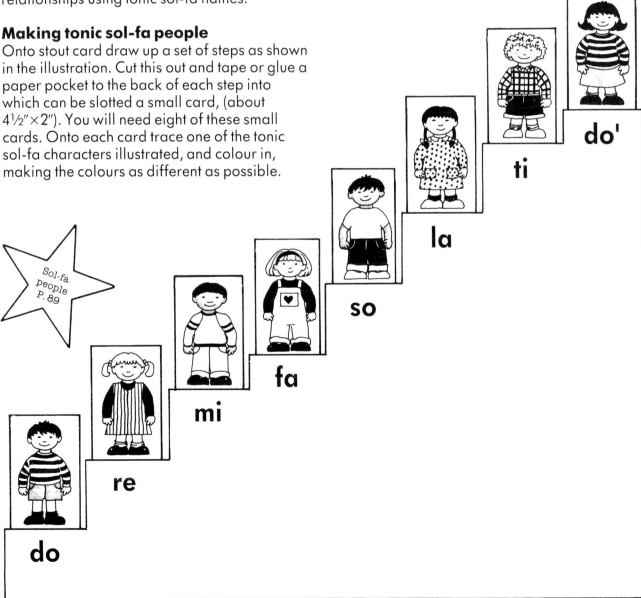

Sol-fa people P. 89

do
re
mi
fa
so
la
ti
do'

Explain that notes on the steps have special names. Sing up and down the scale using tonic sol-fa pointing to the characters as you go. 'Now we are going to meet just two of the tonic sol-fa people.'

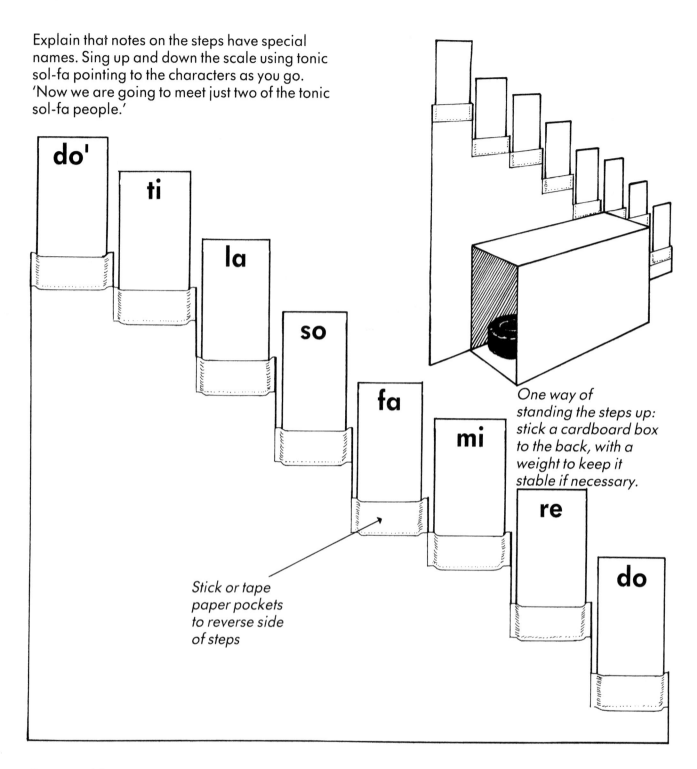

One way of standing the steps up: stick a cardboard box to the back, with a weight to keep it stable if necessary.

Stick or tape paper pockets to reverse side of steps

Reverse side

So-mi

Turn all the sol-fa characters round in their pockets except for **so** and **mi**. Introduce the children to these special singing names and practise singing them. Start with familiar examples of a falling third such as calling out someone's name. (Develop this into a role calls game.) Ask the children how they would call for something ('Mummy, I'm hungry; Daddy, I want a drink of water; Yoo-hoo! Where are you?', etc.)

I personally find hand signs useful with my three and four-year-olds. Although I do not set out specifically to teach *them* to use hand signs at this stage, these signs do act as a visual reinforcement for movement up and down.

Introducing a two-line stave

Rule up a large two-line stave onto which can be stuck large notes cut from black card. Using Blu-tack, fix the cardboard **so** and **mi** characters from the sol-fa family at the beginning of the stave lines, explaining that just as **so** and **mi** have their own special place on the steps, they each have their own special stave line. Stick down the notes, also with Blu-tack, and sing **'so-mi'** pointing to the notes as you do so. Ask the class which is the higher note, and which is the lower.

Don't be afraid to use 'technical' words such as 'stave'. Children enjoy learning new 'special' words (provided that you don't introduce too many at one go!). Show them a piece of 'real printed music' so that they can see the notes going up and down. 'The lines that they go on are a bit like Mr Plinkerton's climbing frame but they have a special name: a stave.'

You may want to explain that a five-line stave is something that people who write music all agree to use: they might need more than five lines in which case they can add extra 'leger lines', or another five-line stave. We don't need all five lines at the moment, so we are just using two.

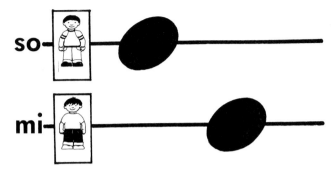

Draw up a large two-line stave and tack 'so' and 'mi' to the beginning of the lines. Cut large notes from black card and tack these onto the stave.

The following little humorous song helped my children to learn the word 'stave' and was extremely popular!

Grizzly bears

Grizz - ly bears live in a cave, But mus - i - cal notes live on a stave, A stave has got five lines you know, And that is where the notes all go! Grizz - ly bears live in a cave, But mus - i - cal notes live on a stave.

Grizzly bears live in a cave,
But musical notes live on a stave,
A stave has got five lines you know,
And that is where the notes all go!
Grizzly bears live in a cave,
But musical notes live on a stave.

Poster 15
P. 80

Activity

Make your own giant musical staves: glue five lengths of string around a cardboard roll; fit a narrower roll, or a pencil inside; ink up the string (black powder paint works fine) and roll away!

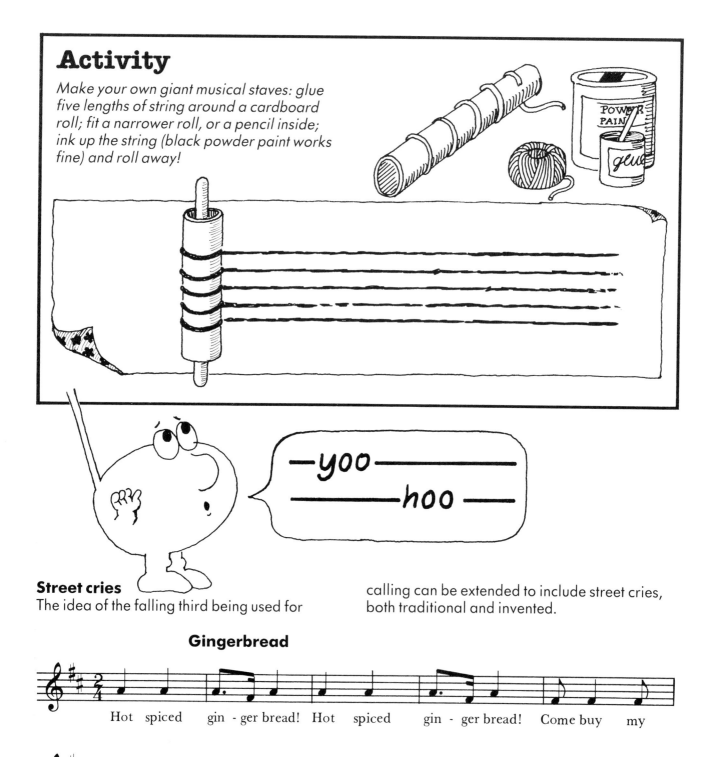

Street cries

The idea of the falling third being used for calling can be extended to include street cries, both traditional and invented.

Gingerbread

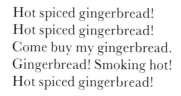

Hot spiced gin - ger bread! Hot spiced gin - ger bread! Come buy my

gin - ger bread. Gin - ger bread! Smok - ing hot! Hot spiced gin - ger bread!

Hot spiced gingerbread!
Hot spiced gingerbread!
Come buy my gingerbread.
Gingerbread! Smoking hot!
Hot spiced gingerbread!

Activity

Set up a table as a market stall and get the children to take turns selling their wares. Encourage the children to make up their own verses, or make them up together.

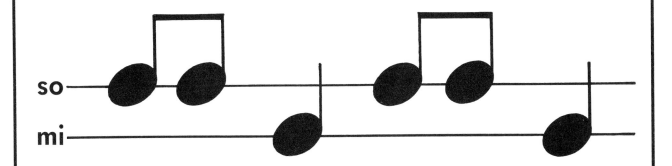

so

mi

Toys to sell

s   s   m   s   s   m
Toys to sell! Toys to sell!

s   m   m   s
Who'll buy my toys?

s   s   m   m   s   s   m   m
Bats and balls and trains and dolls for

s   s   m   m   s
All the girls and boys!

s   s   m   s   s   m
Fish to sell! Fish to sell!

s   m   m   s
Who'll buy my fish?

s   s   m   m   s   s   m
Cockles, mussels, crabs and whelks,

s   s   m   m   s
In a little dish!

The cries do not have to rhyme, but they do need
to be rhythmical. Here are some ideas:

Po - ta - toes! Po - ta - toes! Lots of love-ly po - ta - toes!

An - y old lum - ber! An - y old lum - ber!

Ex - tra! Ex - tra! Read all a - bout it!

Moving out of the market place and into the
busy road, here is something else we can hear
that goes 'so-mi': a police car's siren.

When a police car sounds its siren it's calling
out for other drivers to get out of the way.

Police car

Naa - naa, naa - naa, Driv - ing my po - lice car,

Flash - ing down the mo - tor - way At nine - ty miles an hour!____

Naa-naa, naa-naa,
Driving my police car,
Flashing down the motorway
At ninety miles an hour!

Ding-dong

Ding - dong, ding - dong, Who's ring - ing the bell?

Let's lis - ten care - ful - ly, And see if we can tell.

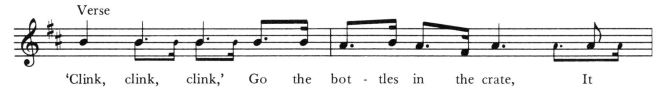

'Clink, clink, clink,' Go the bot - tles in the crate, It

must be the milk - man, Who calls at half past eight.

Chorus
Ding-dong, ding-dong,
Who's ringing the bell?
Let's listen carefully,
And see if we can tell.

'Clink, clink, clink,'
Go the bottles in the crate,
It must be the milkman,
Who calls at half past eight.

Chorus

'Bang!' goes the gate,
Someone's whistling in the porch,
It's the man to read the meter,
With his notebook and his torch.

Chorus

The jingle of a lead,
With a snuffle and a bark,
It's Mary* with her dog,
Because we're going to the park.

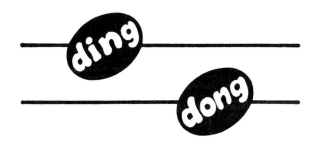

(*Or you can substitute the name of other dog owners in the class.)

Echo games using so-mi

These are just like the rhythm echo games except that for these you sing a short phrase using so and mi. Try the children individually first. If they are ready to attempt singing in unison this will give an opportunity to those who are too shy to sing solo!

It is important to note however that there is a world of difference between lack of confidence and actual inability to determine accurately the pitch of a note. The shy children will need to be drawn out or it will be all too easy for them to sink into the role of the back-row class growler.

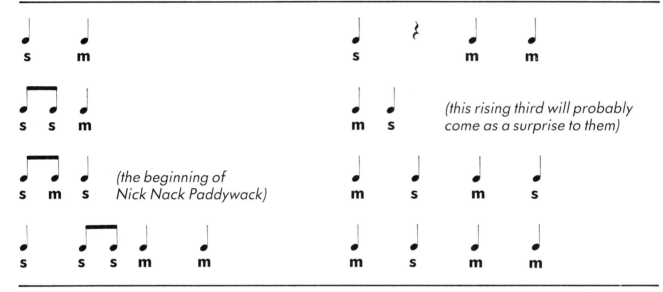

(the beginning of Nick Nack Paddywack)

(this rising third will probably come as a surprise to them)

It is quite likely that one or two children will get the actual pitch wrong but the pitch relationship correct. Listen carefully to their responses. It may be that you are asking them to sing a little outside their own vocal range. Whatever you do do not dismiss a child as 'tone deaf'. This is actually a very rare phenomenon!

Notation idea

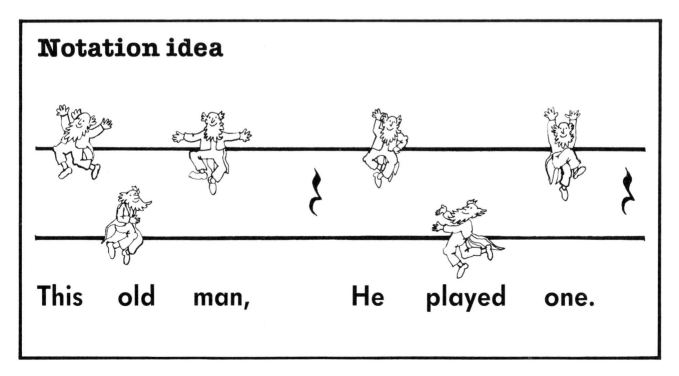

This   old   man,   He   played   one.

Questions and answers: inventing dialogue

Where are you going, little bear?

Q Where are you going, little bear?
A Up in the mountains to get some air,
Q What will you do when you reach the top?
A Come back down with a hop, hop, hop! *hop or skip on these words*

Sowing beans
(old rhyme)

One for the mouse,
One for the crow,
One to rot, and
One to grow.

Children walk round and mime the action of sowing beans.

Dried beans are quite good fun for making rhythms with: Use large beans for quarter-notes (e.g. butter beans) and smaller ones for eighth-notes (e.g. haricot). Lay them out on sheets of thin card or stout paper, drawing in rests where necessary. The beans can be stuck into position if required.

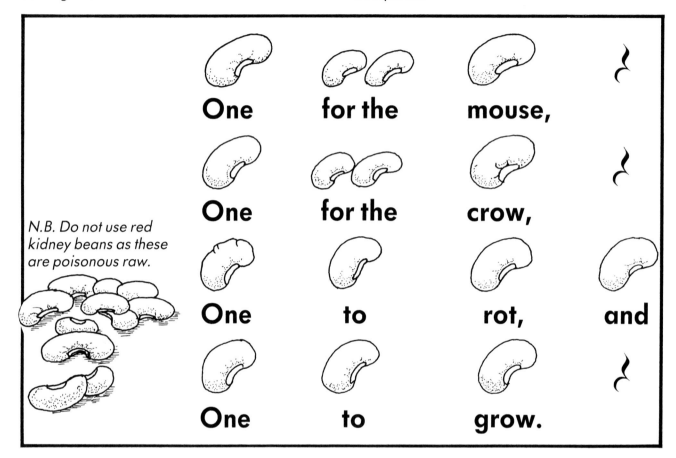

N.B. Do not use red kidney beans as these are poisonous raw.

The following song reinforces so-mi.

Children mime putting a bean into a cup, then make a cup with their hands and finally stretch up high on the last bar.

The movements for putting the beans in the cup should illustrate the movement of so-mi.

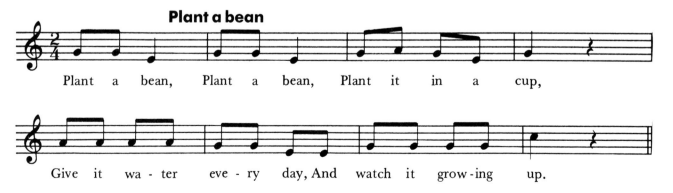

Plant a bean, Plant a bean,
Plant it in a cup,
Give it water every day,
And watch it growing up.

Notation ideas

Make up short rhythmic phrases with beans:

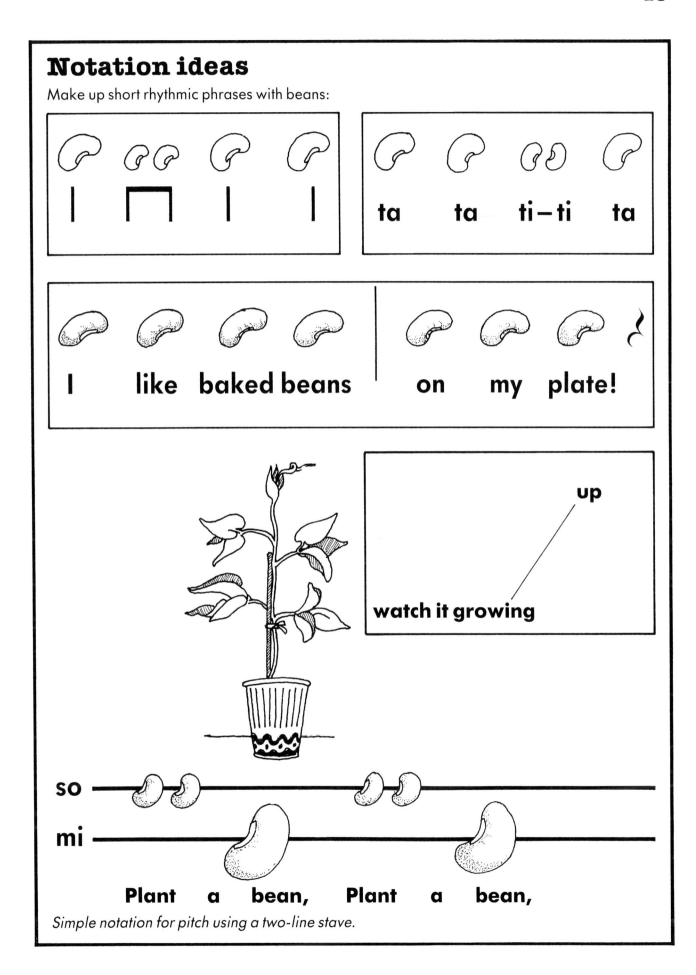

ta   ta   ti – ti   ta

I   like   baked beans   on   my   plate!

up

watch it growing

so

mi

Plant   a   **bean,**   **Plant**   a   **bean,**

Simple notation for pitch using a two-line stave.

In conclusion

I hope it will be seen that to work under a series of headings such as those set out in this book helps teachers to keep aims and objectives in mind and to progress logically with the children according to their ability. I frequently hold a music session around a theme such as the weather, Christmas, movement, jobs, and so on. Using the theme as a starting point I organise the material for the class into the various broad categories of pulse, pitch, rhythm, notation, developing skills, etc. and then slot in any additional material as appropriate.

Whilst I believe it is important to maintain such a methodical approach I certainly would not advocate a totally rigid adherence to any pre-set programme. As long as the basic headings are borne in mind, it helps if the teacher can be flexible and ready to diverge completely from any prepared material if appropriate, in order to respond spontaneously to the needs of the class. I try to have a broad repertoire of songs, rhymes, games and activities ready to hand to cater for those moments that arise spontaneously: a child may throw up an idea that can be developed – perhaps a movement, an invented rhyme or rhythm, or perhaps arrives clutching a precious doll, teddy, or some other toy that may provoke interest and prompt a song. There are always opportunities on which one can capitalise for creating that important element of spontaneity that lends life and colour to any music session. If you can respond to the children's own musical ideas and initiative you increase their confidence in their own ability to make music and to use it as a real and natural language. You demonstrate to them that you accept that their ideas are important too.

Tonic sol-fa
I have found it helpful to introduce tonic sol-fa names as a means of identifying pitch relationships at an early age. An understanding of tonic sol-fa develops a better sense of relative pitch and key mobility as well as fostering a good aural memory and inner ear. For those who do not find the use of tonic sol-fa too daunting a challenge, I would highly recommend Geoffry Russell-Smith's series: *The Russell-Smith Method*, (published by EMI

Music Publishing Ltd) as a logical next step from 'Music with Mr Plinkerton'. Starting at the simplest level, this series develops the use of tuned (and rhythm) percussion with *sol-fa* and singing in a programme of delightful pieces designed to teach reading, playing and listening skills. Attractive piano accompaniments make even the simplest pieces sound like real music. (For non-pianists these are also available on cassette.)

I believe music has a vitally important part to play in the development of any child and that even from the earliest days it is possible to make that something more than just joining in a sing-along or strum-along, pleasurable as these undoubtedly are. If we can train children to really listen intelligently and believe confidently in their ability to do so, we will be laying valuable foundations not only for the musically gifted but for all.

'I hear thunder', with rhythm notation of four quarter-notes, by Joanna, aged 4.

Posters
and
Cards

"Rhythm notation with clapping hands and a person to show you how to do it"

The following section of this book contains a set of posters and a set of cards. It is suggested that the teacher assembles the posters by cutting and pasting the pages together as indicated by the dotted lines. Items on the subsequent pages are for cutting out and pasting down onto card. This section comprises rhythm and signal cards; a Mr Plinkerton to cut out and use with Mr Plinkerton's climbing frame; a set of 'sol-fa people' for use with the sol-fa steps; the sol-fa steps, which are constructed following the instructions on P. 40; and a set of quarter-note rests for use with Poster 11.

I hope that the notation ideas in the posters may inspire both teacher and child to invent his or her own variations. It is my experience that even children as young as three and four are able to grasp the principles of simple rhythm and pitch notation remarkably well and use it imaginatively. They can also get a great deal of fun out of these early steps towards musical literacy.

1

What rhythm are the long legs telling us?

Can you walk it?

What rhythm are the little legs telling us?

Can you walk it?

CUT HERE

What rhythm are the boots telling us?

Can you clap it?

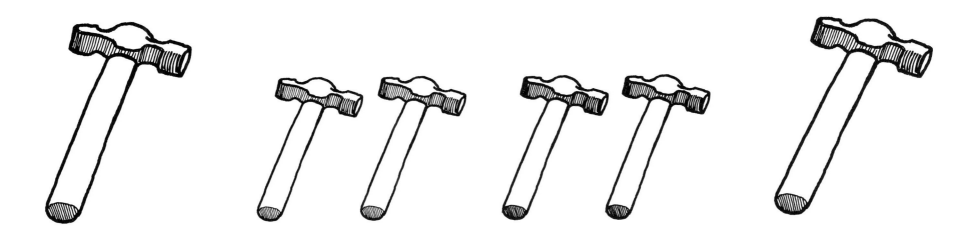

What rhythm are the hammers telling us?

Can you hammer it?

swish swish swish swish

swish swish swish swish

4

Stamp the pulse.

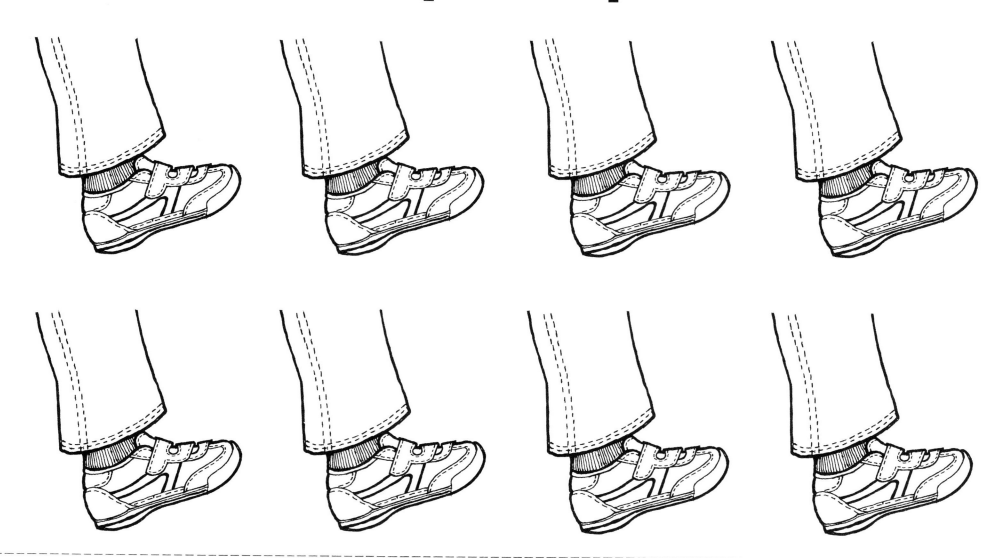

Clap the pulse.

What rhythm are the raindrops telling us?

Can you clap it?

Try whispering 'pitter patter' all the way through the song.

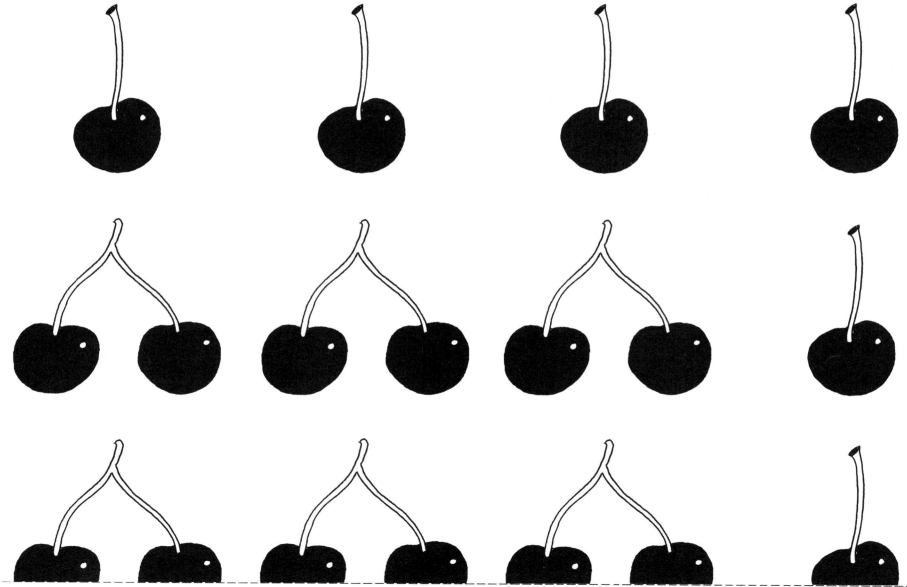

Can you guess the rhyme?

I've got Daddy's slippers on,

Slip, slop, slip, slop,

I've got frogman's flippers on,

Flip, flop, flip, flop,

I've got Mummy's high-heeled shoes on,

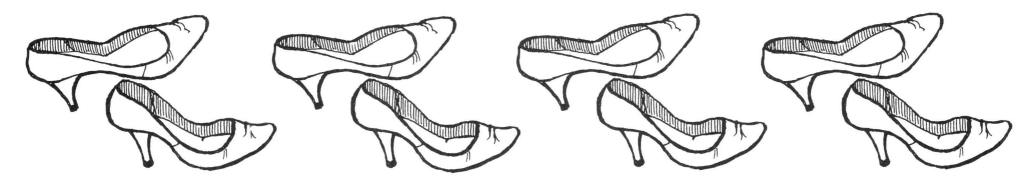

Clit-ter,   **clat-ter,**   **clit-ter,**   **clat-ter,**

I've got Baby's woolly boots on,

Pit-ter,   **pat-ter,**   **pit-ter,**   **pat-ter.**

8

Can you draw a picture of the sounds you hear?

Mr Plinkerton v[...]

Then runs back do[...]

walks upstairs,

wn in case of bears.

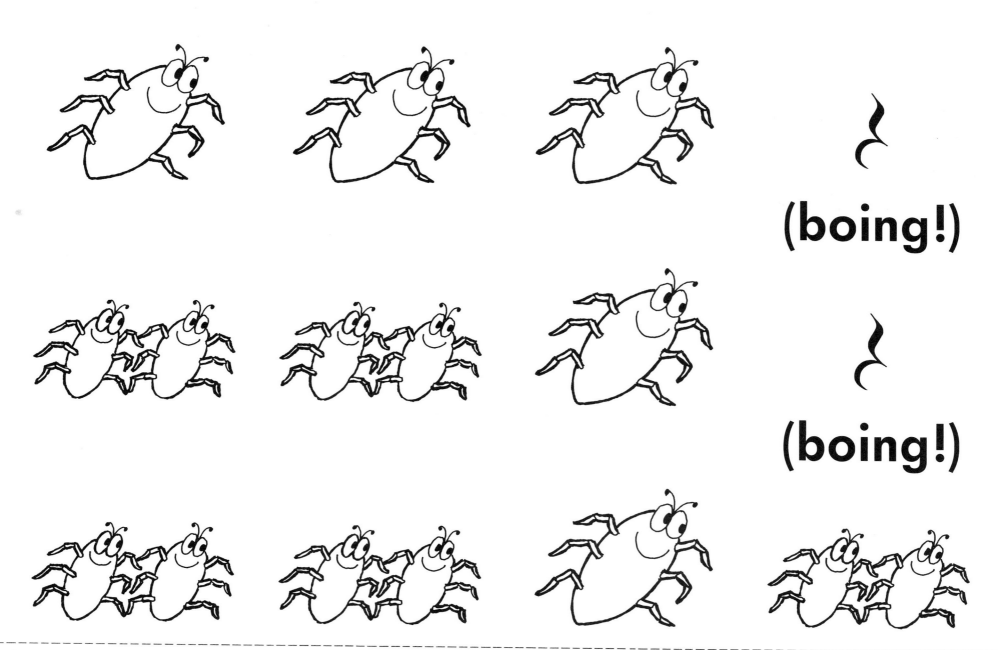

(boing!)

(boing!)

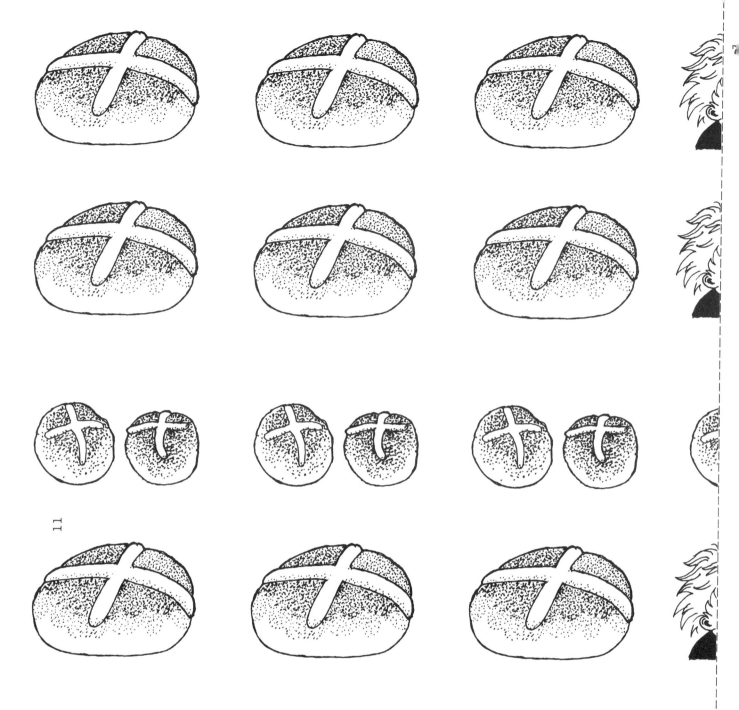

11

What rhythm are the buns tel

Try saying 'ssh' instead of '

ling us?

yum'.

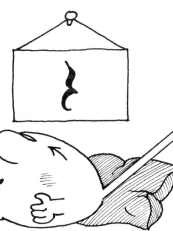

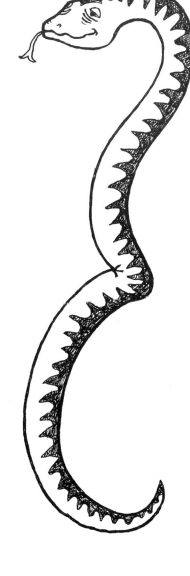

CUT HERE

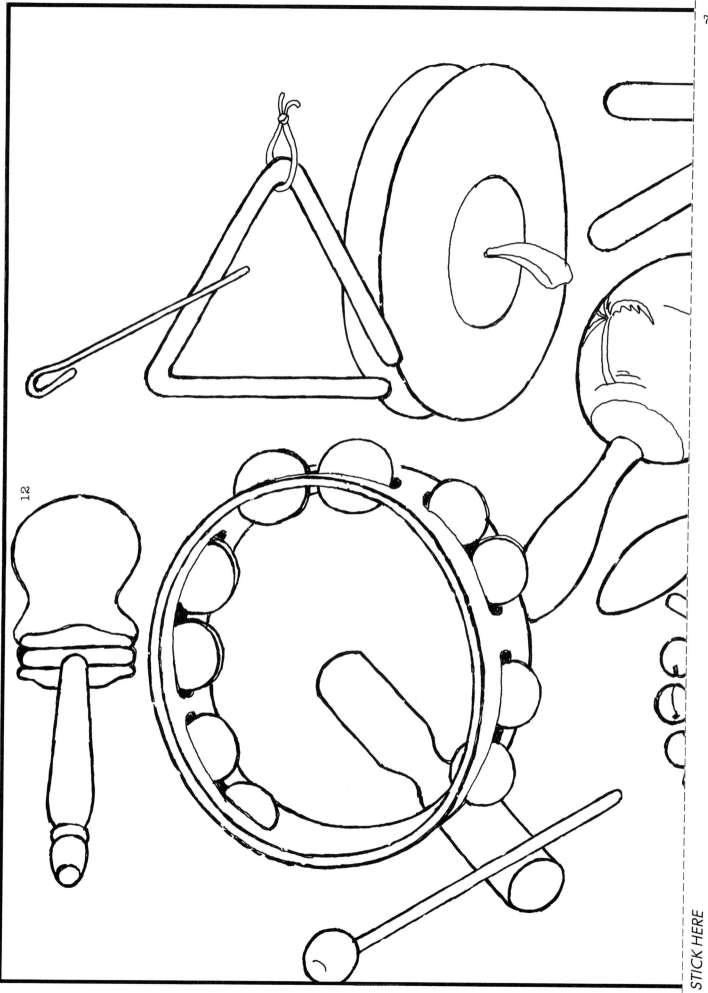

12

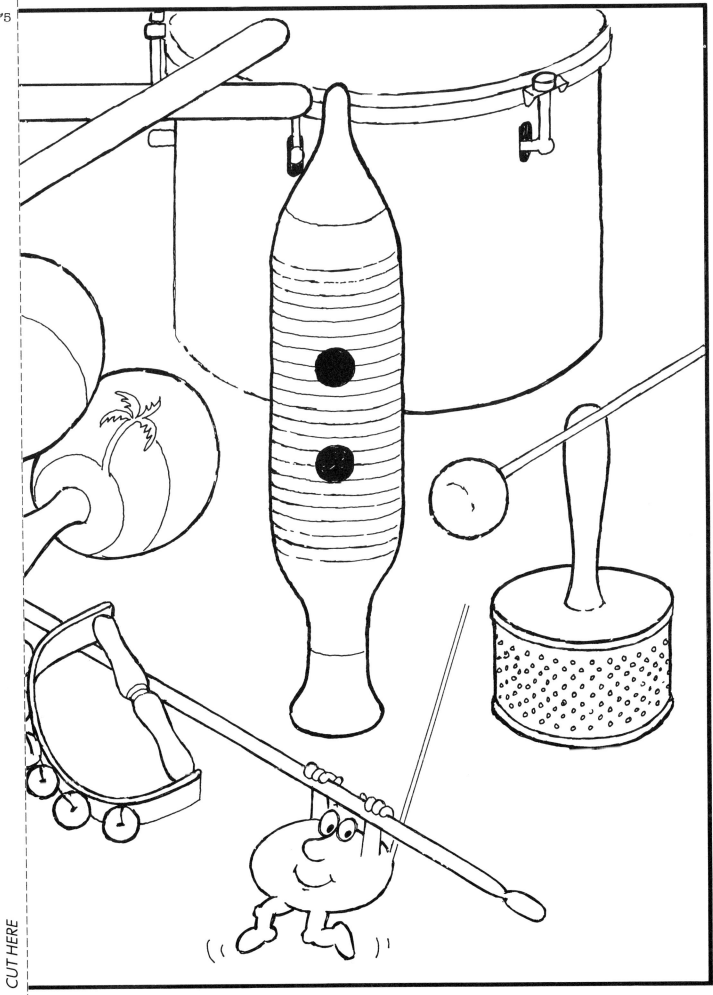

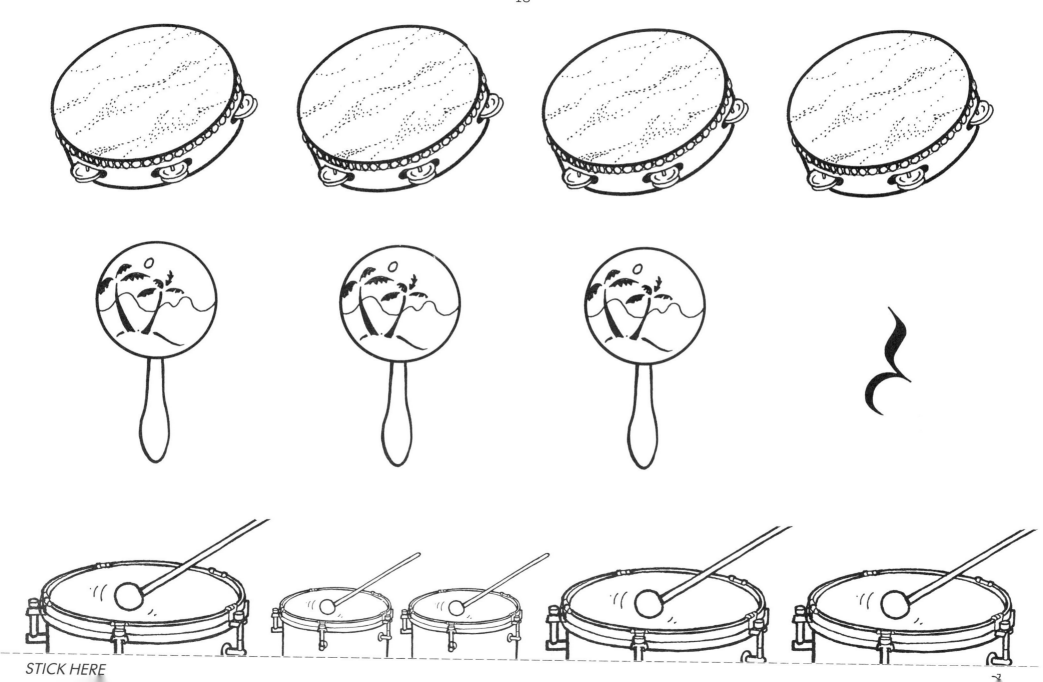

STICK HERE

14

shake   shake   shake   bang

clink   bang   clink   bang

STICK HERE

Grizzly bears live in a cave,

But musical notes live on a stav

*So does
Mr Plinkerton!*

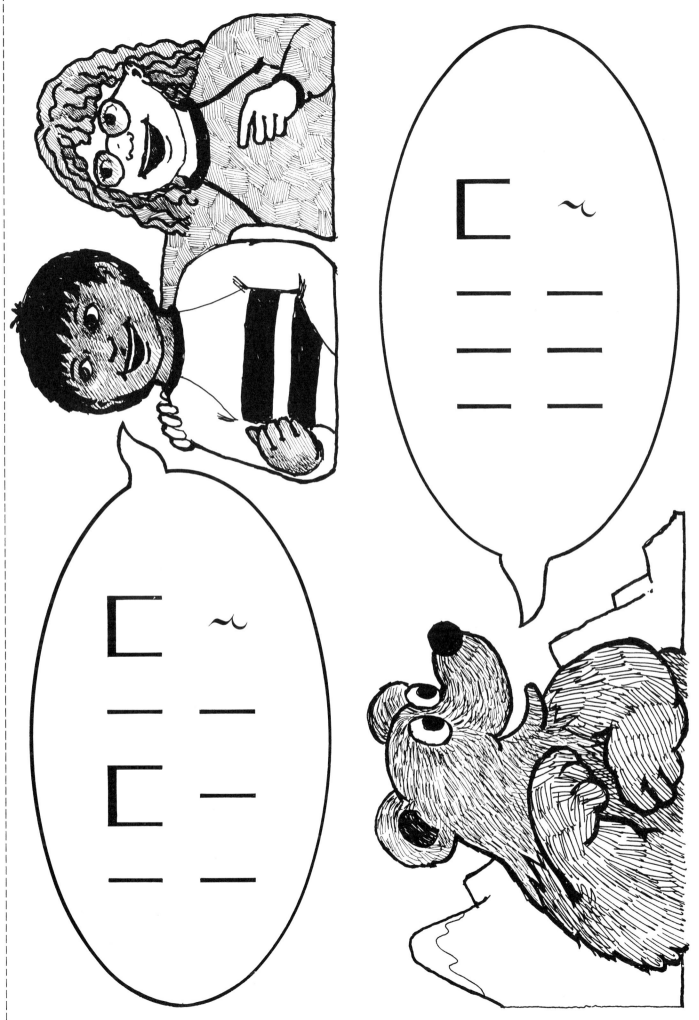

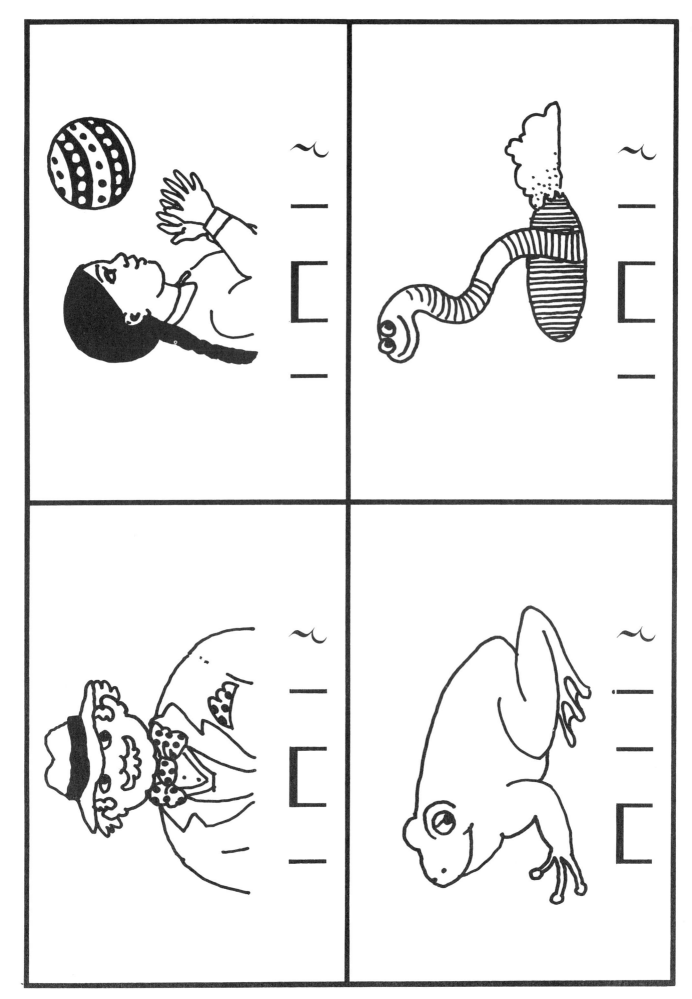

V

Λ

Ϲ

Ϲ Ϲ Ϲ Ϲ Ϲ

Ϲ Ϲ Ϲ Ϲ Ϲ

Ϲ

Ϲ Ϲ Ϲ Ϲ Ϲ

Ϲ Ϲ Ϲ Ϲ Ϲ

87

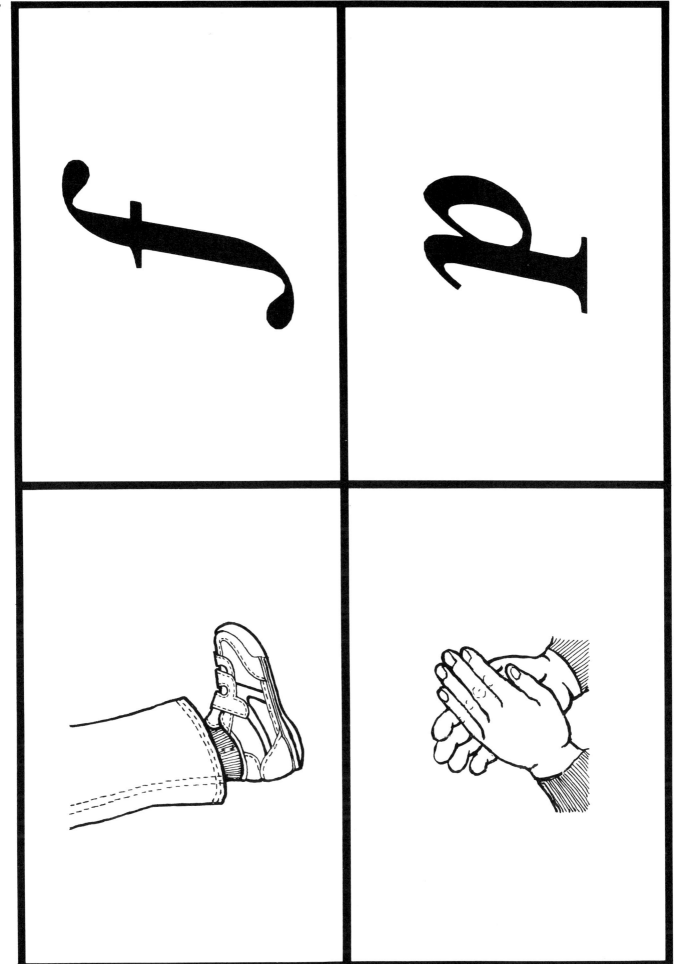

17

do

re

mi

fa

so

la

ti

do'

Index